Jokes For Kids

102 Laugh Out Loud Jokes, Riddles & Tongue Twisters!

Table of Contents

Question & Answer Jokes

1.

Q: What do you call two cats in a fight?

A: A catastrophe!

2.

Q: What bird goes to church?

A: A bird of prey!

3.

Q: What do cows use to do their math homework?

A: Cowculators!

4.

Q: What kind of pie is the best?

A: The one I'm eating!

Q: Why did the worker sit on his watch?

A: He wanted to work overtime!

Q: Why did the elephant wear a coat and hat in the city?

A: He didn't want to be recognized!

Q: What do you get when you cross an alien with a cook?

A: Unidentified frying objects!

Q: What do sheep call their young?

A: Their baaa-bies!

Q: What is brown, cute and has a trunk?

A: An elephant dressed up as a mouse!

10.

Q: What dance does a taco know?

A: The salsa!

11.

Q: Why was one car mad at the other?

A: Because he was driving him up the wall!

Q: How to you keep a gopher from digging up the garden?

A: Hide the shovel!

Q: Why did the queen bee have sticky hair?

A: She used a honey comb!

Q: Why don't centipedes play basketball?

A: It takes too long to put on their shoes!

Q: What did the birdie get when she had a cold?

A: A tweetment from the doctor!

Q: What did the car say to the bridge that wasn't feeling well?

A: What's come over you?

17.

Q: What witch lives in the desert?

A: A sand-witch!

18.

Q: What do you get when you cross a sleepy bull with a tractor?

A: A bulldozer!

19.

Q: What did the girl burger say when she was introduced to the boy burger?

A: Hi Chuck, I'm Patty!

20.

Q: Why does an elephant have a trunk?

A: Because a suitcase would look rather funny!

21.

Q: How can a cat jump higher than a mountain?

A: Easy, mountains can't jump!

22.

Q: What's big and gray, and super noisy?

A: An elephant on drums!

23.

Q: What does a sheep call his house?

A: A sheep shaaaaaaack!

24.

Q: What did one math paper say to the other math paper?

A: You have a lot of problems!

Q: Why did the girl take a ruler to grandma's house?

A: To measure how long it would take to get there!

Q: What do you call young potatoes?

A: Tater tots!

Q: Why did the bunny take the day off?

A: Because he felt jumpy!

Q: What is a grasshopper's favorite game?

A: Hop Scotch!

Q: What did the barber say to the bald eagle?

A: You need to get a wig!

Q: What did the ghost say to the vampire?

A: Brush your teeth – you have bat breath!

31.

Q: Why did the kid swim in the ocean?

A: To get to the other tide!

32.

Q: What do gymnasts eat for dessert?

A: Banana splits!

Q: What do you call a cake that hangs around another cake?

A: A sidecake!

Q: Why did the bull join exercise class?

A: Because he wanted to beef up!

Q: What do you have when you hold 6 apples in one hand and 5 apples in the other?

A: Very big hands!

Q: What shoes do bananas wear?

A: Slippers!

Q: Why wouldn't the tiger play games with the jaguar?

A: Because he thought he was a cheetah!

Q: What bird writes books?

A: A penguin!

Q: What did the germ say to the
other germ?

A: Don't spread my business
around!

Q: What do you call an alligator
who searches for things?

A: An investigator!

Q: Why did the mother bee send her son to a manner's class?

A: So he could learn how to beehive!

Q: What did the orange peel say to the orange?

A: I've got you covered friend!

Q: What do you get when you cross a light bulb with a sheep?

A: An electric blanket!

44.

Q: What did the snail say to the turtle?

A: Slow down, I can't catch up!

45.

Q: What do you call a group of dim-witted skeletons?

A: Numbskulls!

46.

Q: Why didn't the boomerang come back?

A: Because it was bent out of shape!

47.

Q: Why did the boy bury his walkie-talkie?

A: The batteries were dead!

48.

Q: What is black and white again and again?

A: A panda rolling down a hill!

Q: What did one curtain say to
the other curtain?

A: Pull yourself together!

Q: Why does the giraffe have
such a long neck?

A: So he doesn't have to smell
his stinky feet!

Q: What do you call a train filled
with caramel?

A: A chew-chew train!

52.

Q: What happened when the witch went to the Arctic?

A: There was a cold spell!

Mystifying Riddles

53.

What is big, has wings and moves fast, but can't fly?

An ostrich!

What is sometimes there and sometimes not, and depends on water to live?

A rainbow!

What is a foot, has a tongue, but no teeth?

A size 12 shoe!

What has four legs, but always stands still?

A table!

What is round, stands still, but is always moving?

A watch!

What flies in the air and has the same name?

A fly!

What protects as a coat, but sometimes runs?

Paint!

60.

What is hard when cold, and wet
when not?

Ice!

61.

What can't be seen, is sometimes
heard, but has no voice?

The wind!

62.

What has arms and a face, but no
body?

A clock!

63.

What can be seen and felt, but
can't be touched?

The sun!

64.

What can breathe and dance, but
isn't alive?

Fire!

65.

What can be made and broken,
but isn't solid?

A promise!

What has legs, but no feet?

A pair of pants!

What has a head and a tail, but isn't alive?

A coin!

Terrific Tongue Twisters

68.

Thirty-three thistles thickened
their thorns

69.

Share Sherrie's sugary snack
with Sherman

70.

Blake's brown beach balls go bouncing

71.

Sticky stray stickers stay stuck

72.

Gray geese go gathering gallantly

73.

Charlie charged change at Chandler's chocolate shop

74.

Draw different draft drawings
directly

75.

Swimming swans swallow super
salty sea

76.

Ten trained tigers travel too
tirelessly

77.

Strange striking seagulls stare
skyward

78.

Gary's great green glasses glow glowingly

79.

Apes eat cakes and grapes for pete's sake

80.

Fiery fleas fly up and freeze

81.

Roy's toys are annoying noisy noise

82.

Hank was a tank who thanked
and ranked

83.

Keen cans of clams cram in clean
cans

84.

Baby Babbs blows blue bouncy
bubbles

85.

Stinky skunks smell stinky
smelly scents

86.

Sammy saw sally sitting on the seesaw

87.

Cracked crackers crumb crumbs carelessly

88.

Benny was a bitter batter but the bitter batter batted brightly

89.

Frisky cat whiskers feel like sticky stickers

Sixty-six stumps sit still

Rick picked a stick to pick in the
mucky creek

A big black bug bit a brown bear
that bit the black bug back

The bashful cat crashed into a
stash of hash

94.

Which witches wished wishes for fishes

95.

Papa proudly popped a pan of peppery popcorn

96.

Baker bob baked biscuits while buttering bread

97.

Wally walrus watched whales while washing

98.

Shaved sheared sheep are sheepishly shy

99.

Eleven live lions leapt nimbly long

100.

Dark dragons dive and dip diversely down

101.

Ricky fixed dick's mixed mixes

Shellfish sure should see sufficiently sharp

About the Author

Lillie Adams is a fun-loving mother who enjoys being around her kids. They are constantly coming up with funny phrases that inspire her!

Other Books by Lillie

Jokes For Kids: 102 Laugh Out Loud Knock-Knock Jokes!

Jokes For Kids: Another 102 Laugh Out Loud Knock-Knock Jokes!

Jokes For Kids: A 3-in-1 Collection of Jokes, Riddles, Tongue Twisters & Knock-Knock Jokes!

A Laugh a Day: A Write-Your-Own Jokes Diary For Girls

A Laugh a Day: A Write-Your-Own Jokes Diary For Boys